TEACHERS' FAVORITES™

Fun Activities for SPRING!

Reproducible Patterns for Paper Crafts, Coloring Pages, Decorations, and More!

Illustrations by Rick Ewigleben

Publications International, Ltd.

Introduction written by Holli Fort.

Contents

Spring into Action!

It's easy enough to color an Easter bunny or cut out a kite. But having inventive and engaging activities that students respond to, have fun with, and maybe even learn from can be a daunting task. This is true whether you lead a classroom, Sunday school class, scout troop, or a home filled with eager learners. The adaptable projects featured in *Teachers' Favorites*™: *Fun Activities for Spring!* will help you challenge your students with educational activities and purely fun seasonal projects.

Each season in this four-book series offers up a unique buffet of holidays, milestones, sports, and activities. Spring is the time for Easter, Mother's Day, birds, flowers, baseball, and kite flying. Students will enjoy relevant crafts that can be hung, worn, read, laminated, given as gifts, or used to decorate the room or bulletin board.

This book includes the following types of activities:
- Coloring
- Writing
- Math
- Paper crafts
- Games, such as look-and-find, connect the dots, and mazes

For craft projects, take the time to go over the instructions carefully. Also, make sure you have all the materials on hand before you get started. Here are just a few of the materials that are required for most projects:

Paper: Since the projects in this book will need to be photocopied for each student, be sure to have plenty of paper. Most projects can be copied on regular copy paper, but some projects (such as paper dolls and cutouts that stand) should be copied on heavier stock or construction paper. If you do not have access to heavier stock or your copier cannot accommodate construction paper, you can glue the project's paper to construction paper to make it sturdier. For some projects, such as the card for Mother's Day, it is important that you don't see through the paper. In such cases, you might want to glue construction paper to the back of the paper.

Glue and tape: Some projects call for glue and/or clear tape. If you use glue, make sure it is water-base and nontoxic.

Scissors: Many projects call for cutting out pieces. Some require cutting slits or poking holes. For younger children, you may need to do the cutting yourself—or have older children help. Always have safety scissors on hand for smaller hands!

Brads: Some projects call for brass brads to hold pieces together. If you do not have those on hand, you can substitute with twist ties.

Art supplies: Children can use crayons, markers, or paint to color these projects. If children will be painting, be aware that acrylic paint will dry permanently, though when wet it is easily cleaned up with water. Make sure children clean painting tools thoroughly when they are finished painting.

Art smock: Make sure children wear smocks or old shirts to protect clothes while working with paints and other messy materials.

Some children will be able to complete the crafts with little help, but at times your assistance will be needed. Other projects just need a watchful eye. So it is best that you review the project ahead of time and then make a decision about your role.

Flex Time

Another great thing about the crafts, coloring pages, and writing pages in this book is that they provide for versatility—which definitely comes in handy when working with children of differing skill levels. The crafts can be simplified or made more complex depending on need.

Coloring pages are simple enough for younger children, but older children may want to challenge themselves by adding patterns, textures, or even decorations. Likewise, the writing pages are great for older children to let their imaginations flow in creating original stories, while beginning writers may use them to copy a few words or dictate longer stories to an adult. If your group is of mixed ages, consider taking a teamwork approach that combines the imaginative approach of a younger child and the writing skills of an older child.

Great Clips

Clip art pages are great for all kinds of applications. You can use a copy machine to increase the size of the seasonal images to make them suitable for wall or bulletin board decorations. Likewise, you can use the copier to make images smaller for use on worksheets, bulletins, notes to parents, or any other application you can dream up. Incorporate the clip art images to create seasonal birthday cards or stationery, or use them to add a decorative element to any other project.

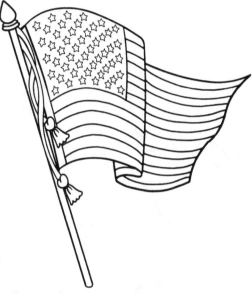

In the Mix

All of the projects presented in this book, from the simplest to the most elaborate, are just ideas to get you started. Feel free to alter the designs by choosing different materials or embellishing in any number of unique ways. Give your imagination free rein as you play around with materials and these base ideas. Encourage students to come up with their own unique variations on these themes, and keep them in mind for later uses. You can jump off in any direction, keeping these projects as fun and fresh as the first time you tried them. When it comes to creating fun springtime activities, the sky is the limit!

Spring Is Here!

March Holidays

The Robin's Nest

After spending the winter down south, many species of birds head back north when the weather warms. In the spring, birds build nests and lay eggs. Have fun coloring this scene of a robin and her chicks!

Flying Birds

Cheer up the classroom with colorful, flying birds! Color and cut out each pattern. Cut slits and punch holes where indicated, and then insert the wings. Connect the birds to the branch with string and watch them fly!

Bee-lieve It!

There's a lot of work to be done! Help this confused honeybee find her way out of the beehive so she can gather nectar with the rest of her crew.

Answer on page 96.

What's Your Middle Name?

Middle Name Pride Day is celebrated on the Friday of the first full week in March. Write your first, middle, and last names on the nametag. Write your middle name big so that everybody can see it. (If you do not have a middle name, choose one that you would like to have!)

Hello, My Name Is...

———————————————

———————————————

———————————————

My Favorite Breakfast

National School Breakfast Week is celebrated every March to make kids aware of the importance of a good breakfast. Which of these foods do you like for breakfast? Color your favorites, cut them out, and place them on your dish and placemat. Enjoy your hearty meal!

March Madness

March is time for playoff basketball. Add up all the sums in the basketballs. Then put that total number in the home team's part of the scoreboard. Let's hope the home team wins!

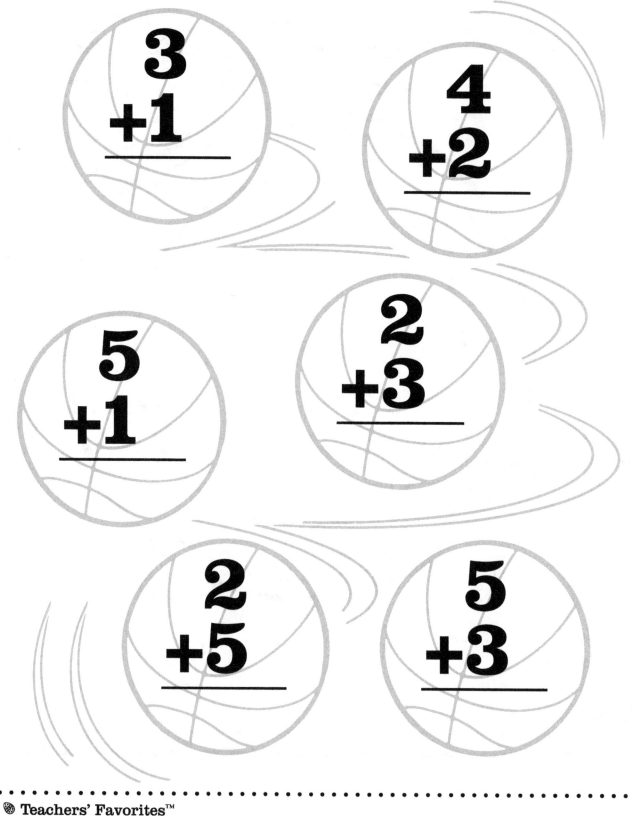

$$\begin{array}{r} 3 \\ +1 \\ \hline \end{array}$$

$$\begin{array}{r} 4 \\ +2 \\ \hline \end{array}$$

$$\begin{array}{r} 5 \\ +1 \\ \hline \end{array}$$

$$\begin{array}{r} 2 \\ +3 \\ \hline \end{array}$$

$$\begin{array}{r} 2 \\ +5 \\ \hline \end{array}$$

$$\begin{array}{r} 5 \\ +3 \\ \hline \end{array}$$

VISITORS

HOME
TEAM

35

GO
TEAM!

MARCH
MADNESS

Answer on page 96.

Outside Fun

Things I Like to Do Outside

_____

_____

_____

_____

_____

_____

_____

Slow Movin'

Help this snail along by connecting dots 1 through 13. Color the finished picture.

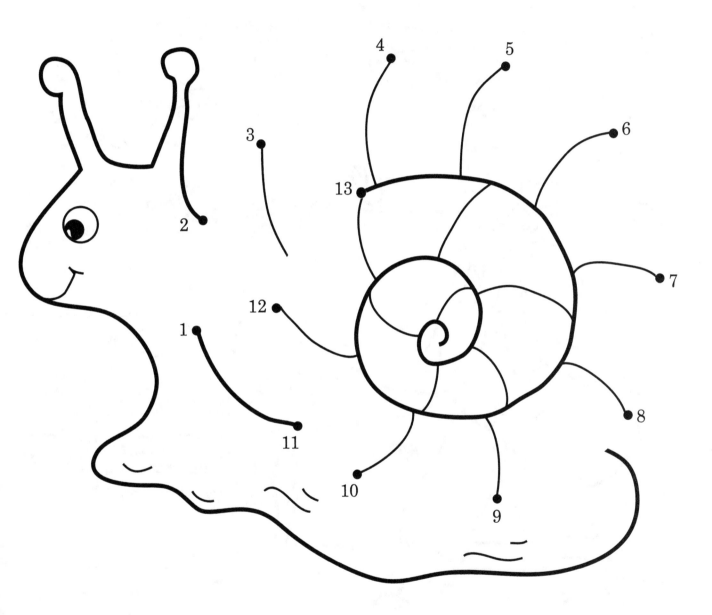

Johnny Appleseed

March 11 is Johnny Appleseed Day. Color this scene while learning the tale of the man who helped plant apple trees across much of America.

A Is for Apple

Write down other words that begin with the letter A.

St. Patrick's Day

St. Patrick's Day is held on March 17. Pull out your crayons and make this leprechaun's dream come to life!

Best Wishes

According to tradition, if you find a four-leaf clover, you make a wish. What do you wish for?

I Wish For...

_____

_____

_____

_____

_____

_____

_____

_____

You, the Artist!

March is National Youth Art Month. Use this
blank canvas to express your creativity!

Home Fixes

Can you find 10 or more errors in this scene?

Answer on page 96.

Dancing Leprechaun

Make a leprechaun dance! Color and cut out the head, torso, and four limbs. Then use fasteners to put the leprechaun together. Sing a song and watch him dance!

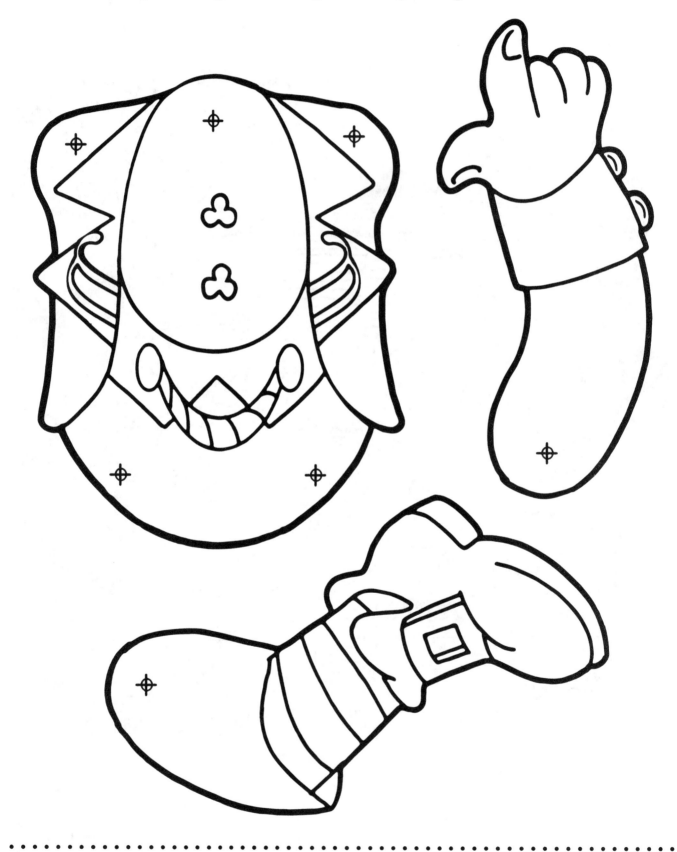

Pot of Treasure

While the leprechaun searches for a pot of gold, we found a pot of treasure just for you! Can you add the numbers on these coins to determine how much money you have?

Answer on page 96.

Flower Power

Help this flower grow by connecting dots 1 through 33. Color the finished picture.

Answer on page 96.

In Like a Lion...

According to an old saying, March "comes in like a lion and goes out like a lamb." Discuss what that saying means. Then color, cut out, and fold these patterns to create a standup lion and lamb.

∙∙∙∙∙In Like a Lion∙∙∙∙∙

...Out Like a Lamb

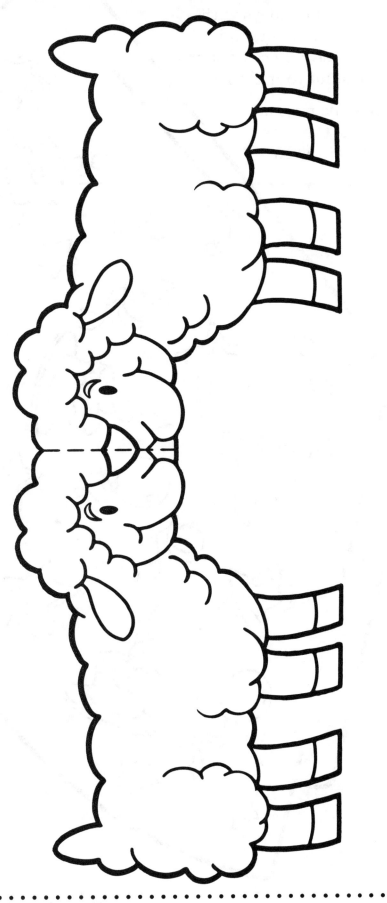

A Birthday Hat

Celebrate this month's birthdays with this festive hat.* Color, cut out, and fasten the hat. Then use a piece of string to secure the hat around your chin.

* Teacher: Enlarge this page at 150 percent to make the hats big enough for the children.

All-About-Me Quilt

March 21 is National Quilting Day. Fill out and color this all-about-me paper quilt.

Springtime Crossword

Look at the pictures on this page, and name each one. Then write the word in the correct numbered spaces.

Across

1.

3.

5.

6.

Down

1.

2.

4.

Answers on page 96.

Make a Splash!

Happy Easter!

April Showers Bring May Flowers

The rain that falls in April helps our flowers grow. Color and cut out the clouds, tulips, and daffodils. Punch holes where indicated. Use thread or string to attach the clouds and flowers to a hanger. It's the perfect "rainy day" activity!

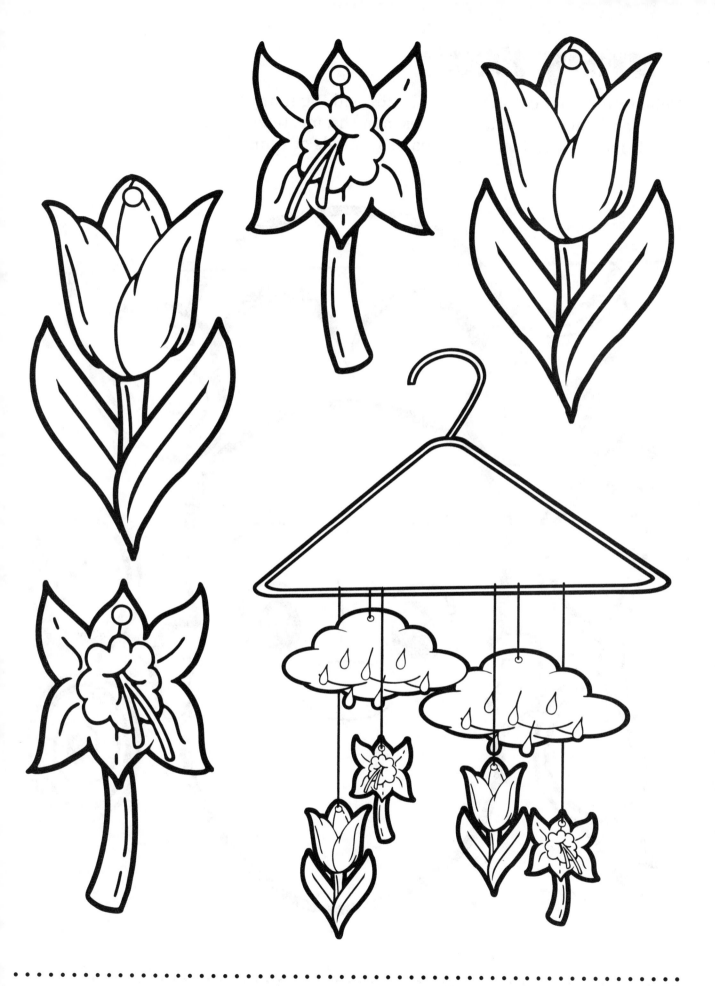

Funny Face

Celebrate April Fool's Day (April 1) by making funny faces.
Color and cut out the hair, glasses, mouths, mustache, and beard.
Try different combinations to make all kinds of funny faces.

Laugh Out Loud!

On these lines, write some funny jokes. They can be jokes
you have heard or those you make up yourself.

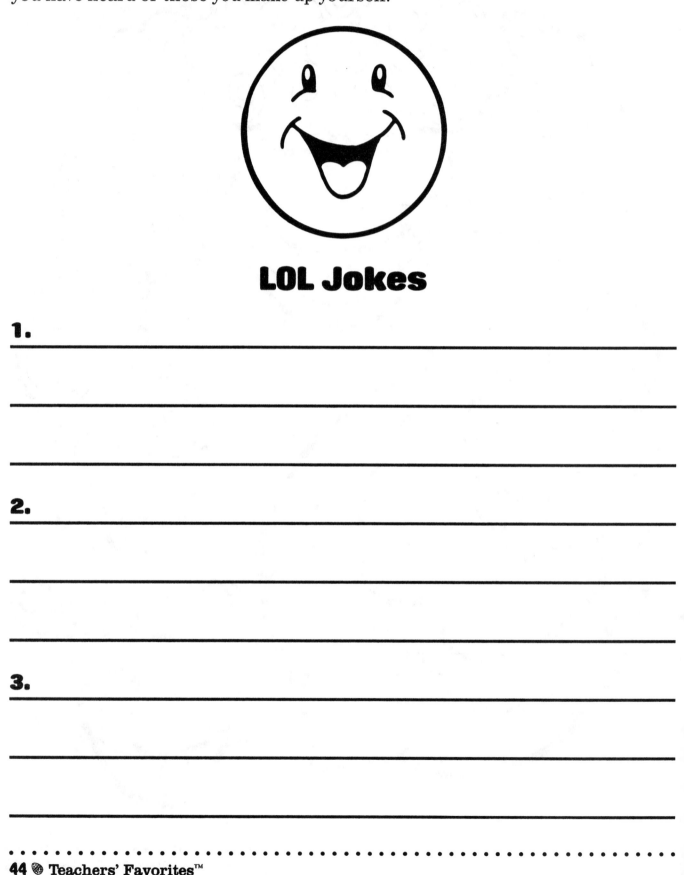

LOL Jokes

1. _____

_____

_____

2. _____

_____

_____

3. _____

_____

_____

It's Raining, It's Pouring

Look at the pictures on this page, and name each one. Write the word in the correct numbered spaces. Be sure to check to see if the word should be written across or down.

Across

3.

6.

Down

1.

2.

4.

5.

Answers on page 96.

Prepare the Firefighter

Can you dress these firefighters to get them ready for their next mission? Color and cut out the firefighters and their clothes/accessories. Fold the tabs to secure the clothes on the figures' bodies. The accessories can be glued or taped. Now they are ready for action!

Rainy Day Fun

Things I Can Do on a Rainy Day

1. _____

_____

2. _____

_____

3. _____

_____

4. _____

_____

Cut out the entire picture below. After coloring the items, paste the whole picture on the side of a box. You will then have a "Rainy Day Box." Fill it with toys and other fun things that you can play with on a rainy day.

Standup Easter Eggs

It's time to design Easter eggs! Color the eggs and then cut them out.
Examine the diagram to learn how to create your own standup Easter eggs.

Easter Basket

Color this Easter basket and cut it out. It will make a festive holiday decoration for your classroom or home.

Easter Egg Glasses

It's time to get a little silly! Color and cut out these Easter egg glasses and put the pieces together. You'll need to tape the "hinges" so that the glasses will be secure enough to wear.

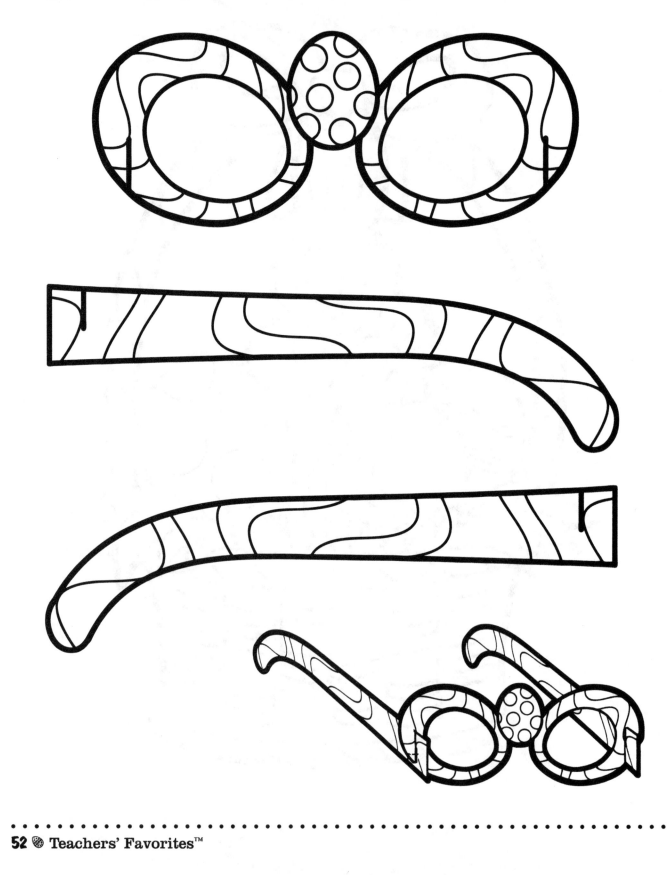

Standup Easter Bunny

Color, cut out, and fold this pattern to create your own standup Easter bunny.

Easter Egg Hunt

Hidden in this picture is a bunch of Easter eggs. Try to find as many as you can. Finding 20 or more would be *egg*-citing!

Answer on page 96.

Count and Color Jellybeans

April 22 is National Jellybean Day. Color all the jellybeans in the jar with six different crayons: red, blue, purple, green, yellow, and orange. How many red jellybeans are there? Write that number next to the word *Red*. Do the same for the other colors. Add the six numbers. How many total jellybeans are in the jar?

Red _____

Blue _____

Purple _____

Green _____

Yellow _____

Orange _____

Total _____

Answer on page 96.

What's in *Your* Garden?

April is National Garden Month. Color and cut out all of the vegetables and fruits, then place them in the garden. Which ones are your favorites?

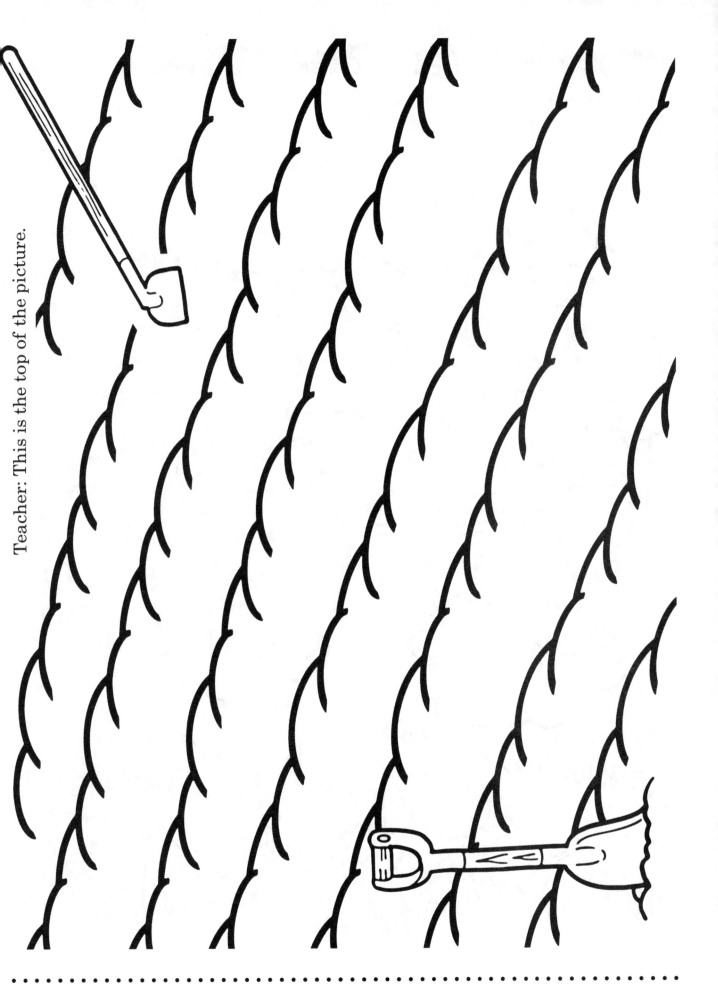

Teacher: This is the top of the picture.

America the Beautiful

April is Keep America Beautiful Month.
Have fun coloring this beautiful park scene.

Birthday Badge

Color and cut out this birthday badge. Don't forget to write your age on the middle line. Attach to your shirt with a piece of rolled-up tape.

I Am Years Old

Fly a Kite

April is National Kite Month. On a windy day, go outside and fly one. In the meantime, cut out and color this mini kite. Add ribbon for a tail.

Kick It!

It's April, and that means it's time for spring soccer season. Color this
kickin' scene. Later today, maybe you could play the game for real!

Celebrate Earth Day

April 22 is Earth Day. On this day, we learn how to take care of our environment and conserve Earth's resources.

On the globe below, color in the continents and oceans.

On the right-hand page, color the household objects. Then cut out the objects and the words. At home, you can tape them in appropriate places as reminders to save energy.

Lamp

Turn off the light when you are not in the room.

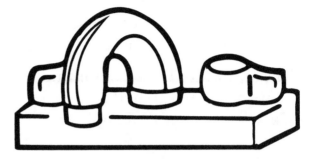

Faucet

Turn off the faucet while brushing your teeth.

Recycle Bin

Paper, plastic, and aluminum garbage goes into the recycle bin. (Check first with a parent or caregiver!)

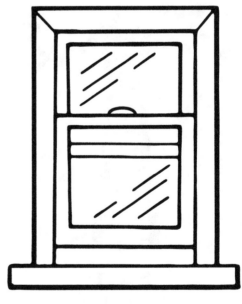

Window

Close the windows when the heat or air conditioning is on.

Arbor Day

The last Friday in April is Arbor Day. On this day, people are encouraged to plant trees. Why? Because trees provide cleaner air, food for animals and people, shade on hot days, natural beauty, and more.

On this page, color in the oak, palm, and evergreen trees.

On the right-hand page, color and cut out the shapes to make your own evergreen tree and apple tree.

Oak

Palm

Evergreen

Get a Jump on It

Hop to it, and connect dots 1 through 61. Color the picture when you're done.

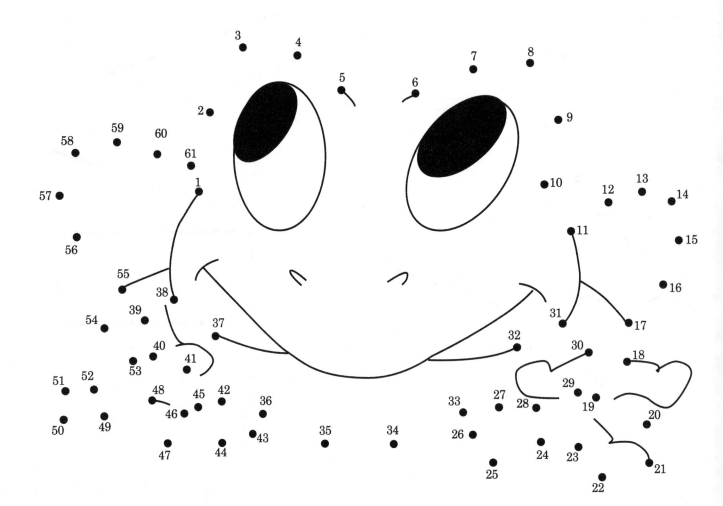

Answer on page 96.

Days to Celebrate

Happy Mother's Day!

Cinco de Mayo

On Cinco de Mayo (May 5), Mexican heritage and pride are celebrated.

On this page, color and cut out the sombrero and maracas, two symbols of Mexican culture. On the right-hand page, color the outfits of the children, who are dressed up for Cinco de Mayo.

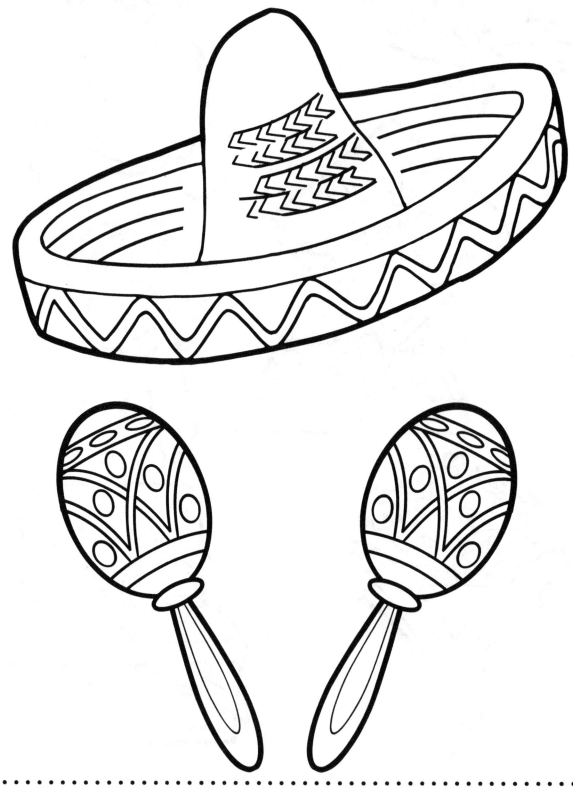

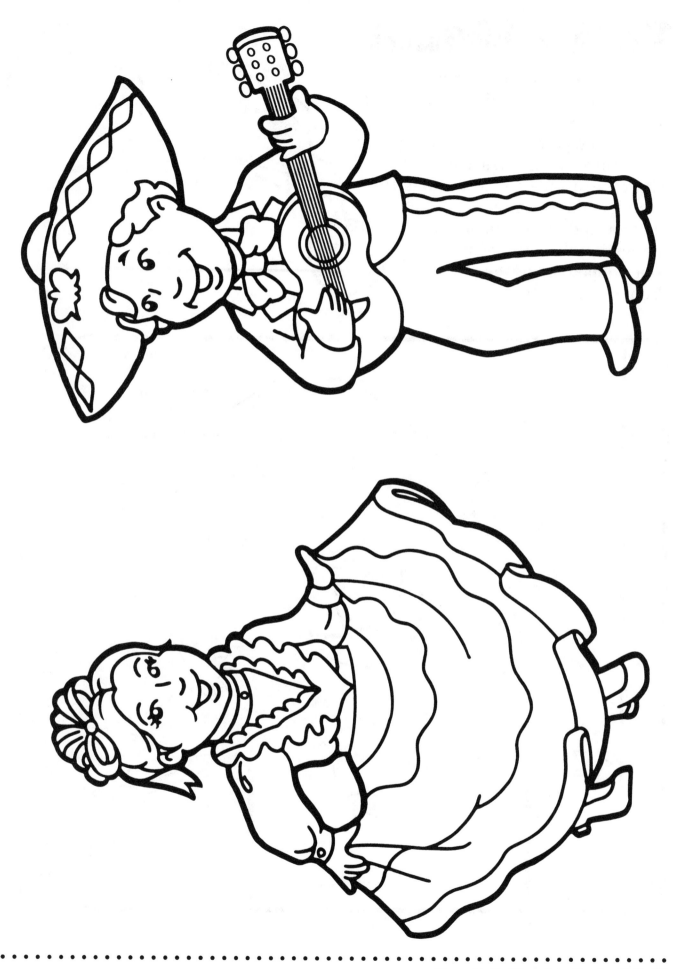

To the Moon!

Are you ready to build a three-dimensional rocket ship? It's easy. First, color the pieces of the rocket ship. Cut out the patterns. Turn the pattern below into a cylinder, securing it with glue or tape. Cut slits along the straight lines of the cylinder and the fins, and insert the fins. Turn the semicircle pattern into the cone-shaped top of the rocket. Prepare for blastoff!

finished project

Mother's Day Card

Why buy a Mother's Day card when you can make one yourself? Cut out the card's cover and interior pages. Paste the pages on the back of the card, and fold. Color the cover. On the writing lines, list all the things you love about your mom or caregiver.

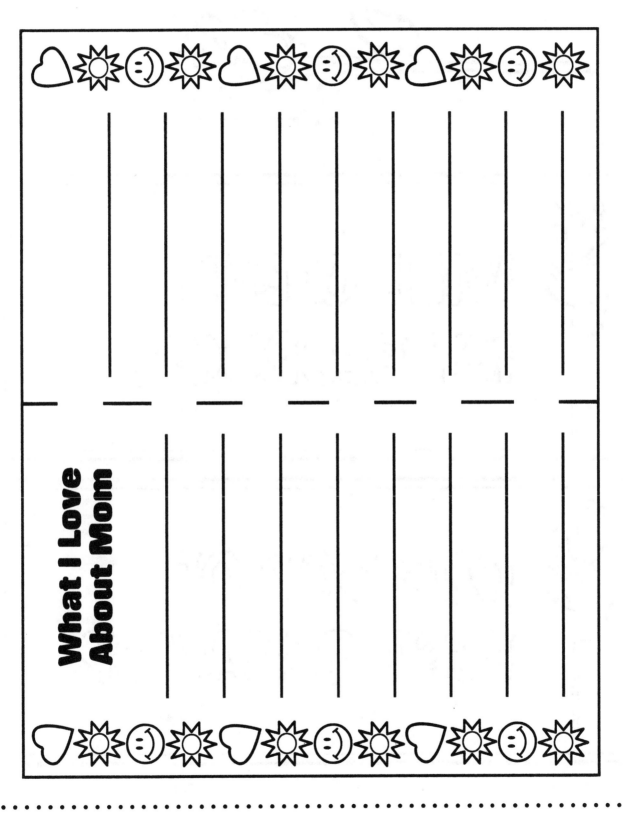

What I Love About Mom

Mother's Day Coupons

Here is a gift that Mom is sure to love! Cut out these coupons and present them to your mother or caregiver. You might want to include them in a Mother's Day card. Be sure you live up to your promises!

WILL CLEAN MY BEDROOM

ONE DAY OF BEST BEHAVIOR

WILL HELP WASH DISHES

WILL TAKE OUT TRASH

WILL READ A BOOK TOGETHER

A Picture to Cherish

Find a great photo of you and your mom or caregiver. Cut out the middle of this frame, and paste or tape the photo to the back of the frame. Once you color it, you'll have a great Mother's Day gift!

Mom and Me

Choo-Choo!

National Train Day is celebrated every May.
Color and cut out this classic train engine.

A Good Day for a Picnic

With the weather warming up, May is a pleasant time to enjoy a picnic. You can have a pretend picnic in the classroom. Color and cut out these pictures and the picnic basket, and place the items in the basket.

Be Kind to Animals

Be Kind to Animals Week is celebrated in early May. Color this barnyard scene. Be sure to give a pat on the head to the horse, donkey, sheep, duck, rabbit, and goat!

Amusement Park

You won't need a ticket to visit this wacky amusement park! Test your powers of observation by completing the following activities. Don't use the same answer twice.

1. Find 5 things that begin with the letter *R*.

2. Find 3 long, thin things hidden in this picture.

3. Find 5 other things that don't belong in an amusement park.

Answers on page 96.

Make a Book

Reading Is Fun Week is celebrated each May. Here is your chance to write something fun. Write a poem that rhymes and a poem that is just plain silly! Cut out the cover and the pages, and then paste them together to create your own book.

My Book of Fun Poems

By _____

:)

Published by Rhyme Time, Inc.

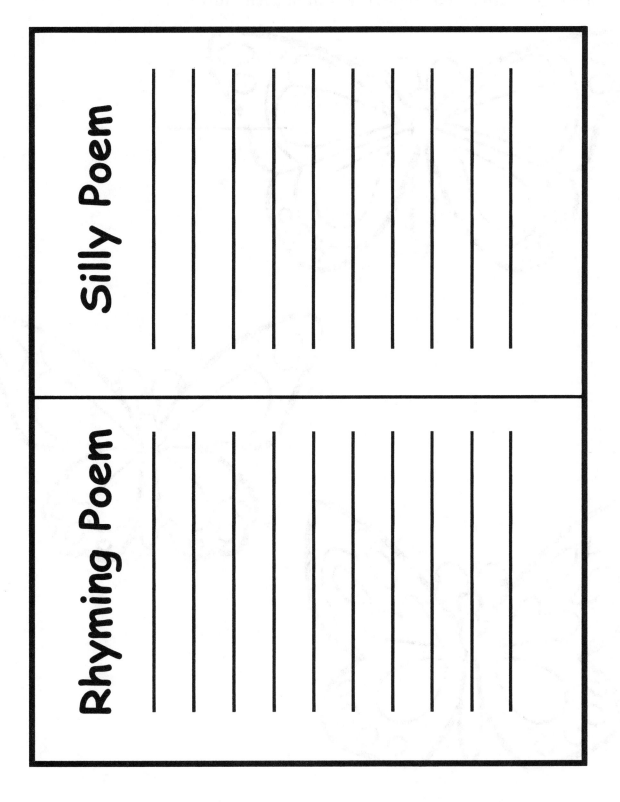

Silly Poem

Rhyming Poem

Fluttering Butterflies

With crayons and creativity, you can make these butterflies beautiful! When you are done coloring, cut out the butterflies and punch smalls holes in the top-middle of each. Hang the butterflies from a hanger with thread or string. Watch them flutter!

Pizza Party!

National Pizza Party Day, held every May, is a great reason to celebrate. Color and cut out the pizza as well as the toppings. Then place your favorite toppings on your pizza. Delicious!

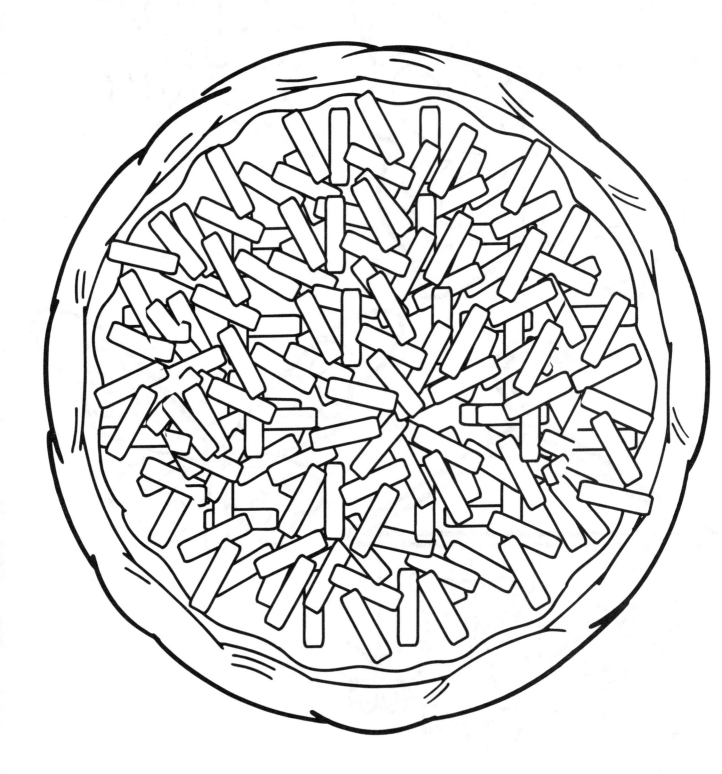

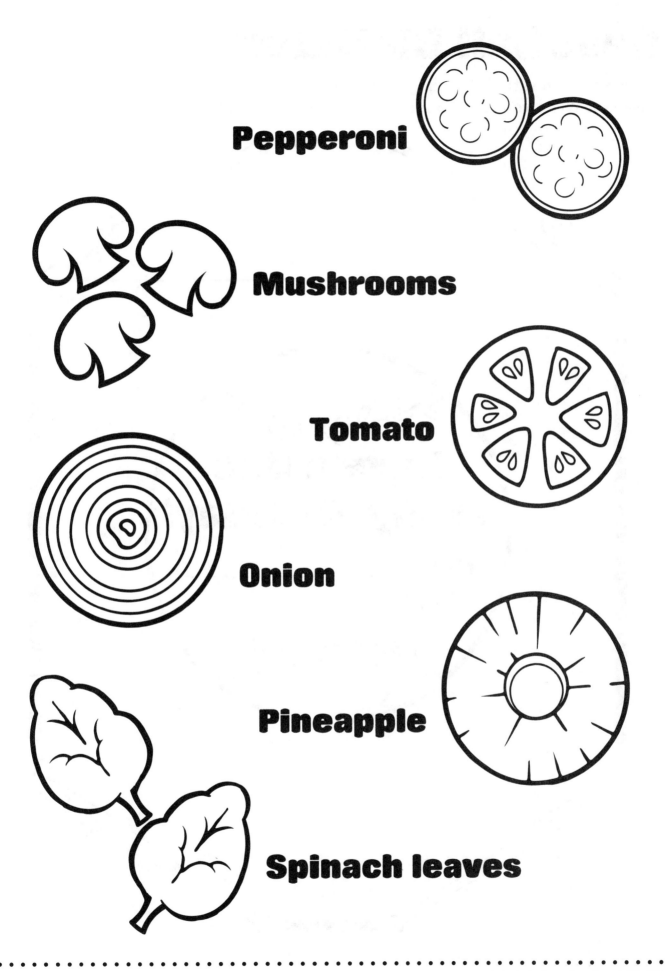

Pepperoni

Mushrooms

Tomato

Onion

Pineapple

Spinach leaves

Baseball Birthday

By coloring the stitches red, you can create a birthday badge that looks like a baseball. Write your name and birthday on the lines. Wear the badge with pride!

Have a Ball
on My Birthday!

Name: _____

Date: _____

Zoom! Zoom! Zoom!

The Indianapolis 500 auto race is run on the day before Memorial Day.
Color and cut out this cool Indy-style racecar.

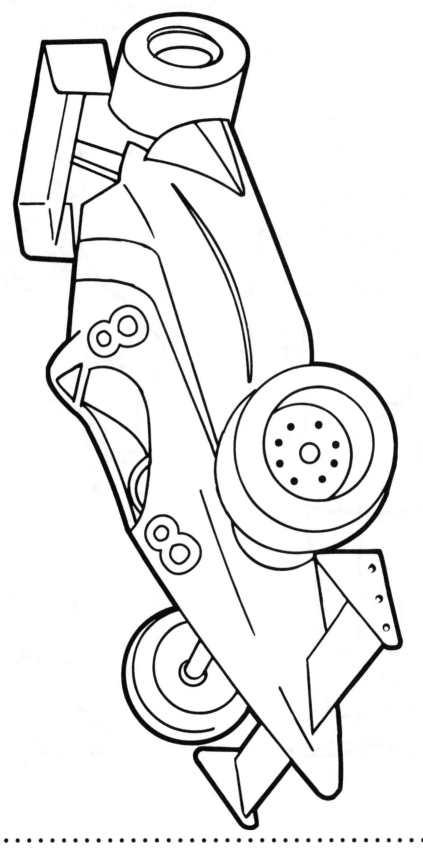

Prepare a Police Officer

National Police Week is celebrated every May. It is a great time to honor our country's police officers. They often put themselves in harm's way to protect us. In this fun activity, you get to prepare the police officers. Color and cut out their clothes and accessories. Use the flaps to fasten the clothes onto the officers' bodies. The accessories can be glued or taped.

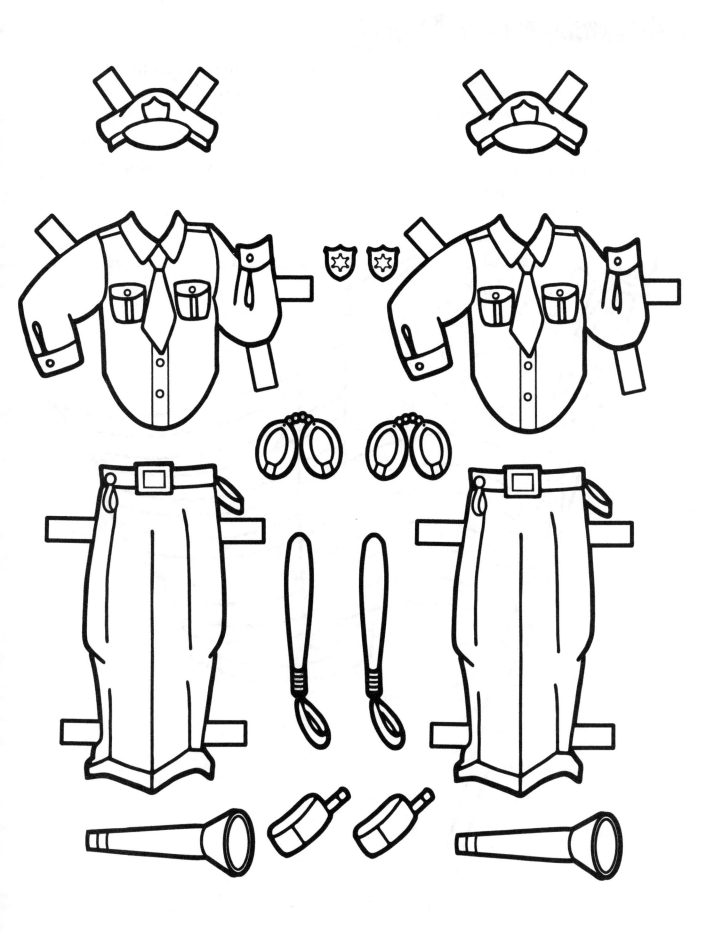

Memorial Day

Memorial Day is held on the last Monday in May. On this special holiday, we honor the American men and women who have died while serving in the military. In many communities, parades are held on this day.

Color and cut out the flag below. You can display it in the classroom or bring it home with you. On the right-hand page, color the servicewoman and serviceman, who are marching on Memorial Day.

Answers

Bee-lieve It! *(page 14)*

Flower Power
(page 31)

Easter Egg Hunt
(page 54)

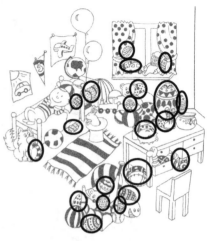

March Madness

(pages 18–19)
The home team's total is 36.

Slow Movin'
(page 21)

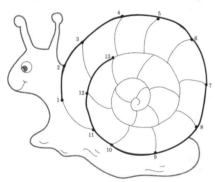

Home Fixes *(page 27)*
1. car; 2. chimney; 3. doorknob; 4. jump rope; 5. lawnmower's wheels; 6. missing "5"; 7. tree's leaves; 8. wagon's handles; 9. water from hose; 10. weather vane (to name a few).

Springtime Crossword *(page 36)*

It's Raining, It's Pouring *(page 45)*

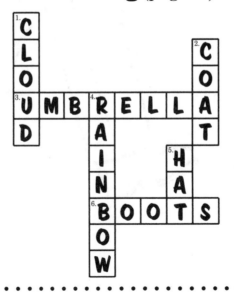

Count and Color Jellybeans *(page 55)*
The total number of jelly beans is 56.

Get a Jump on It
(page 66)

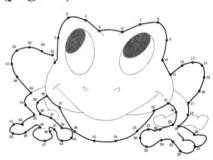

Amusement Park
(page 83)
1. These start with R: radio, ruler, rabbit, ring, rake.
2. These are hidden: pencil, baseball bat, spoon.
3. These don't belong: cow on Ferris wheel, lawn mower, chair, frying pan, telephone.